PREMILLENNIALISM EXPOSED

JOHN METCALFE

Printed and Published by
John Metcalfe Publishing Trust
Church Road, Tylers Green
Penn, Buckinghamshire

—

First Published November 1986

—

ISBN 870039 05 X

—

Price 25p

—

CONTENTS

PREMILLENNIALISM EXPOSED

PREMILLENNIALISM EXPOSED

Premillennialism

THE word premillennium is a compound word made up of a prefix and a noun. The prefix 'pre', meaning 'before', refers to the coming of Christ, indicating that the second coming of Christ is 'before' what is described in the last part of the word. The last part of the word, the noun 'millennium', has reference to 'a thousand years'. Hence the complete word indicates the second coming of Christ before 'the thousand years'.

2. The Thousand Years

What thousand years? One might well ask. The answer is that there is a certain view which teaches that Christ will come again to reign on earth for a thousand years. This scheme depends entirely upon a literal interpretation of one allegorical passage of scripture, and one only. In that place alone, Rev. 20:1-7, one reads of 'a thousand years' in such a connection, although the connection is so tenuous that the second coming of Christ is not even mentioned in these verses.

1

3. The Old Testament

Thousand years reign? In the Old Testament it is true that the word 'thousand' occurs frequently, but never once is it used to refer to a thousand years in connection with Messiah's future reign. The Hebrew for 'thousand' is *eleph* and this might well suggest the elephantine blunders of a system of eschatology without a basis in scripture. One reads of a thousand hills, a thousand vines, a thousand Philistines, a thousand children of Bigvai, a thousand Ammonites, a thousand spears, a thousand camels, a thousand horses, a thousand chariots, a thousand judges, a thousand bullocks, a thousand rams, but never of a thousand years reign, no, not from Genesis to Malachi.

One can discover a thousand shields for a thousand Israelites, a thousand cubits and a thousand footmen to traverse them, a thousand talents and a thousand oxen to carry them, a thousand silver pieces and a thousand Edomites to covet them, a thousand baths and a thousand men to bathe in them, but what no one can find, no, not one of a thousand, is a thousand years reign at the end of time with the second coming of Christ preceding this millennial invention.

However, at last having gone through all the thousands in the Old Testament, climbed a thousand hills, drunk a thousand flagons, taken a thousand baths, viewed a thousand cattle, and examined a thousand officers, one finds a thousand years in Psalm 90:4. Here, a thousand years are in the sight of God as yesterday. Not tomorrow, prefixed by the second coming. Of course Solomon refers to a thousand years twice told, in Eccl. 6:6, which amounts to two thousand, and in it, the wise man finds no good.

But, out of every reference to a thousand, and the two or three to a thousand years, in the whole Old Testament, a man will be hard put to knock together one single sentence of gleaned words that will give a reason for the hope of premillennialism, to justify it according to the oracles of God.

And if that be the case with the Old Testament, how much more with the New?

4. The New Testament

The Greek word for 'thousand' is *chilias*, and by the foolishness of preaching the spiritual fulfilment of Samson's slaying a thousand with the jawbone of an ass shall be fulfilled through the grace of God in this tract.

The only reference to a thousand years—apart from the highly allegorical and spiritualised passage in Rev. ch. 20 —in the entire New Testament, appears in II Pet. 3:8. This passage, the only clear and direct passage in the whole Bible to the return of Christ in connection with a thousand years, teaches the direct opposite to the premillennial scheme.

There were those who murmured at the delay in the return of Christ, the long-awaited second advent appeared drawn out, they said 'Where is the promise of his—second —coming?'

Peter rebuked them, saying the delay was not long. Why not? Because one day is with the Lord as a thousand years, and a thousand years as one day. That explains why the interval is drawn out—in the judgment of men—before the second coming of Christ. But the 'thousand years', or divine day, for however many 'days' it may be, is before the Lord returns, not after it!

Their scheme is in the very teeth of plain scripture and clear doctrine, so that to justify what they foist on scripture, they depend on obscure passages, not one of which—save the allegorical Rev. 20—contains the words 'a thousand years', much less does it connect such a period with the return of Christ.

5. Revelation Chapter 20

Obscure passages, symbolic usage, allegorical imagery, on this the premillennialists depend to place the thin end of their wedge in the Bible. Of course it must be the book of Revelation. Of course it must be Revelation 20. Into that, they force every veiled prophecy from the Old Testament, every strained interpretation of the book of Daniel. Just as, obstinately, they will not treat the prophetic references to Israel in the Old Testament in a spiritual way, so, with equal perversity, they refuse to accept the allegorical language of Revelation chapter 20 other than in the most literal manner.

4

But this is a folly, clean contrary to the use of numbers in the book of Revelation. We read of seven candlesticks, seven horns, seven eyes, seven angels, seven churches, four beasts, twenty four elders and seven seals. They themselves know that none of these numbers is literal. They admit this, for the simple reason that to deny it would be to appear ludicrous. Then, if numbers are to be spiritually interpreted in the beginning and throughout the book, by what rule will they make an exception at the end of it, in one of the most highly allegorical passages of all?

In the Apocalypse there are four horses, one penny, a little season, a sevenfold judgment, one hundred and forty four thousand, three woes, a third part, four angels, one hour, one day, one month, a third part of mankind, two hundred million lion-like horses on fire, seven voices, seven thunders, forty two months, one thousand two hundred and sixty days, three and a half days, seven thousand slain men, twelve stars, seven heads, ten horns, a time and times and half a time, seven beast-like heads with ten horns, two lamb-like horns on a single beast, and the number six six six.

The book speaks of one thousand six hundred furlongs of blood, seven last plagues, seven vials of wrath, seven mountains, three unclean spirits like frogs, a dragon, two beasts, a false prophet, a whore that is a city, and a city that is a whore, seven mountains which become seven kings, five of which were fallen, one of which existed, and the last still in the future, the beast being the eighth which was, and is not, and is yet to come.

There appears a sevenfold conqueror with three names, eyes of fire, an unknown name, a sword coming out of his mouth, riding in the sky on a white horse, covered with blood-soaked clothing, and followed by armies in heaven on white horses. He fights against the nations and kings of the earth led by a seven-headed beast with a false prophet, in turn directed by a dragon, who is a serpent, who is two spirits, who has seven heads, ten horns, seven crowns, and a tail. And this spiritual, symbolic figure is to be bound by a visible angel with a literal chain in an actual pit with a material cover for a factual thousand years?

Do they ask us to believe that this figure is intended to be taken literally, against the entire tenor, scope, method and system of the book? And if they do, where is the second coming in Rev. 20:1-7? Where are the Jews? Where is Jerusalem? Why are the thrones in heaven? Why 'souls' not persons? That they have got away with this scheme in evangelicalism for so long is a clear indictment of the state of christendom, a plain indication of the need for the axe to be laid to the root of the trees, or ever we shall come back to our measure of what was in the beginning. And, remark, this small tract deals with the matter in little more than the briefest of ways.

However, enough is said to show beyond reasonable doubt that a scheme dependent upon the notion of a thousand years reign after the second coming of Christ, named premillennialism in consequence, cannot show one single explicit, didactic text naming a thousand years from the whole bible to justify the myth of Christ's millennial reign. Much less can premillennialists connect such a notion with the second coming of Christ in any one place in scripture.

6. The Interpretation of Revelation

Their entire interpretation of the book of the Revelation is untenable. According to their view the church is 'raptured', or secretly raised from the dead—ten thousand times ten thousand, and thousands of thousands, and myriads besides, from the north south east and west, from the land and from the sea, 'secretly' raised from the dead? —as indicated in Rev. 4:1.

Revelation 4:1? But the 'come up hither' was not spoken to the church in the future, but to John at the time. It is not in the plural 'you', but in the singular 'thou'. It is nothing to do with the church, but was entirely to do with the writer, as the events show.

In their scheme the body of the book, from chapters four to nineteen, is neither to do with the church, nor with this age. Then why write it to the church, in this age? At the end of this period, the so-called tribulation period, Christ is supposed to return, suspend the entire church over the earth, and descend from them to reign, glorified, upon the earth amidst the corruptible and mortal Jews at Jerusalem for a thousand years.

The fact that neither the Lord's return, the church's return and suspension, the Jews, Jerusalem, or any suchlike

things are mentioned in this allegorical passage—Rev.
20:1-7—gives the premillennialist no difficulty. Of course
not, because already he has had to undo fundamental
doctrine, overturn plain scripture, outrage proper principles of interpretation, and force conceptions foreign to
the tenor and sense of Holy Writ to such an extent, that
there can be no difficulty in the final issue.

Undo fundamental doctrine? Overturn plain scripture?
When is this? Where is it? I will tell you.

The basic principles of interpretation of type and
prophecy teach us that the Old Testament must be understood in the light of the New. Only the plain, clear,
didactic teachings of Christ and the apostles can elucidate
those obscure prophecies of the former prophets necessarily
couched in language suitable to the then-revelation of the
mind and ways of God. How could the Old Testament
writers speak in New Testament terms of what is explicitly
called 'the revelation of the mystery hidden from ages and
from generations'? They could not. But they could, and
did, use the language proper to their times to speak—
without understanding what they said—of things to come.

Thus the prophetic utterances, visionary allegories,
imagery and graphic types of the Old Testament must be
subject to the fulfilment of the New, and to the plain
apostolic teaching of things to come. Only clear New
Testament teaching can open up the mysterious passages
in the prophets speaking of future blessings for the people
of God after the coming of Christ. Any prophecies, any

passages on the promises to Abraham and to his seed, must be cast in the light of New Testament revelation.

Furthermore, even in the New Testament, pictorial imagery and allegorical figures must be subjected to clear doctrine, not the other way round. For example, the book of Revelation is expressed in terms of graphic, vivid imagery. But II Peter chapter 3 is written to give the most unambiguous doctrine. Then, the former is to be interpreted in the light of the latter, and must be subject to that light, without equivocation.

Another important principle of interpretation regarding prophecy is that of parallelism. This is consistent, it holds good throughout the prophets, as it does in the Revelation. The prophecy recurs over the same period, say, from the first to the second advent, again and again, but from a different elevation. Premillennialism ignores and goes clean contrary to these principles.

Premillennialism reverses these principles, collating the promises to Abraham and ignoring Paul's interpretation of them in doctrinal terms: collecting the prophecies concerning the Jews and ignoring their spiritual fulfilment in the church. Left with the amassed texts from these two sources, they go straight from the Old Testament to a mystical, figurative book, Revelation, capable of being made to say anything simply because it is so full of figurative imagery.

Ignoring the plain teaching upon the last times and events in the New Testament, they drop their two groups of texts from the Old Testament into the hole they create in Revelation 20, and, wonder of wonders, premillennialism is proved.

Their opponents are ridiculed, the Reformers are incomplete men, the Nonconformists were quaint individualists. Church history—till Lady Powerscourt's meetings of the premillennial aristocracy—was in obscurity. But they are the ones that are in darkness: they ignore, spurn, and reverse the correct norms of scriptural principles of interpretation.

7. The Secret Rapture

They are really unscriptural. Revelation 4:1, which they say is a secret(!) resurrection from the dead, is in fact no more a rapture than their feverish imagination is spiritual interpretation. Firstly, it is in the first person, not the third, therefore to John, not the church. Next, the words 'Come up hither' were fulfilled in John, who was then caught up. And finally, the reference to the first resurrection in Rev. 20 is denied, because Rev. 4:1 would have been the first resurrection.

Furthermore, if that were Christ's second coming for his own, why is he not mentioned in the chapter? Ch. 4 reveals a mysterious vision of Almighty God, not Christ's coming to raise and rapture the church. Almighty God appears on the throne of glory, Christ, as Saviour, is not seen, only John is caught up, no resurrection is mentioned, and what was spoken of occurred to John then and there.

But the premillennialist has his scheme, his bagful of Old Testament prophecies, his misconceptions of I Thess. 4, and now the scripture must be rent somewhere to drop these notions into the breach. It starts at Rev. chapter 4 and slides down to chapter 20. Who but blind men and blind followers could get themselves into this hole?

8. The Great Tribulation

Revelation chapters 4 to 19 therefore—according to them—has nothing to do with the church. But if Rev. 4:1 were the church being raptured, being glorified, actually seeing Christ on high, why is John required to write down what Christ himself in person could tell them face to face in glory, things that will follow on earth after the church's departure into heaven? Sixteen chapters of events that do not concern them? During which they are with Christ in heaven?

The premillennialists confine these chapters to what they themselves admit does not concern the church, about a state through which it is not to pass, during which it abides with Christ glorified in heaven, thereby using up sixteen—irrelevant—chapters from a book of but twenty-two chapters all supposedly written for the edification and comfort of the church!

During this period, when the church is supposed to be raptured—that is, Rev. chapters 4 to 19—the premillennialists pretend that events on the earth point to a multitude of Jews being converted in the great tribulation, as they call it.

Converted? But not to the gospel once delivered to the saints. No, another gospel, preached by angels, is supposed to convert them.

'But though we, or an angel from heaven, preach any other gospel unto you than that which we have preached unto you, let him be accursed.' 'Which is not another, but there be some that trouble you.' That is, premillennialists, who trouble the Jews with another gospel.

Again, the Holy Ghost is supposed to have been withdrawn with the church. So the Jews, converted by an accursed angel having another gospel, are brought to God, they say, by 'him that willeth', by the power of the flesh. But the flesh, saith the apostle, profiteth nothing, flesh and blood cannot inherit the kingdom of God, and, 'it is not of him that willeth'. If it were, God would be obliged to reward human merit, the strength of the flesh, and the will of man, and hence the reward would not be of grace, but of debt. And where is the divinity in that?

Furthermore, they would be converted for no other reason than that they were Jews. Then, he is the God of the Jews only. If so, faith is made void, and the promise of none effect. This is to overturn the grace of God with a witness. Well, why has not somebody said so?

In the premillennial scheme, circumcision gains currency with God, and it is a question of the flesh, that is, Jewish flesh. Salvation is now by genealogy, 'Conform to the Jews and thou shalt be saved' is the watchword, and

Annas' and Caiaphas' only mistake was to have been born in the wrong generation. Though perhaps premillennialism, infatuated by circumcision, will save them also, along with Ananias and Sapphira.

So that, without the Holy Ghost, by Jewish merit, circumcision profiteth much, and the blessing, of works, is upon the Jews only. Paul's writings are overthrown, free grace is trampled underfoot, the cross, with the body of sin resurrected, is annulled, and God's everlasting covenant made of nothing worth.

How is this? A rent has been made in the page of Holy Writ, a hole has been torn by the hand of man, vast collections of irrelevant texts have been dropped in, out of context and at random, but all is well because it is not the gospel dispensation. No, it is a hole, a black hole, torn in time and space. And by this imaginary mutilation they can overturn every principle of grace established in the New Testament?

9. The Millennium

I come to Rev. 20:1-7. This is supposed to be the thousand years millennial reign of Christ. The raptured and glorified church is supposed to be suspended over the earth, hovering so as to block out the sky, inert for a thousand years, whilst Christ reigns, glorified, amidst a people full of inbred sin, in the body of sin and death, in the flesh and blood which cannot inherit the kingdom of God. It is not merely that this is ludicrous, fantastic to the point of bringing the laughter of the ungodly upon all that is holy, it is iniquitously wrong in its mixture, the very thing God hateth.

Christ is, meantime, supposed to reign at Jerusalem. Yet in this passage his return is not mentioned. Not once. Jerusalem is not mentioned, no, not until the 'thousand years' are over! As to reigning at Jerusalem, not a word is said.

As to the godly reigning, souls that were beheaded, and those that had not received the mark of the beast, lived and reigned with Christ a thousand years. Nothing whatever is said of the Jews, nor of the earth. They are souls, not in the body, they are not said to be on earth, on the contrary as souls they reign with Christ in heaven.

For—in heaven, Psalm 2:6—he must reign, till he hath put all his enemies beneath his feet, I Cor. 15:25. This is the reign, and those are the thrones, seen in another figure in Rev. ch. 5, the thrones of the twenty four elders. These answer to the thrones of judgment in spiritual Zion, Psalm 122:5. This is the fulfilment of Psalm 110, 'Sit thou at my right hand, until I make thine enemies thy footstool.' The last enemy, Rev. 20, is Satan and his power, death.

Here Christ is on high, Phil. 2, 'God hath highly exalted him.' And the souls of the saints with him, Eph. 1, 'seated with Christ in heavenly places'. If so, on thrones. Now. It is seated, not 'to be seated'. 'To him that overcometh will I give to sit with me on my throne.' These things are fulfilled in the souls of those that, having overcome, depart to be with Christ in glory.

14

Chapter 20 occurs in the context of one of the seven parallel sections in the book of the Revelation, that showing the destruction of the devil, and of death. This began with the first advent, and will be concluded at the second.

At the cross the devil was destroyed spiritually. In the ascension, Christ and the saints reign over all, which reign is called figuratively '1000 years'. This is no more to do with reigning in Jerusalem over the Jews on earth in a fictitious future age than it is to do with Aesop's fables. Less.

It is altogether to do with Christ's reigning now from the glory in the present age, set forth in symbolic figures, using the threefold multiple of ten, in terms of the longest unit of time. That is, the number of divinity, three, the number of completeness, ten, multiplied in fulness, and expressed in terms of time. This symbolises Christ and the saints' reign in glory throughout the age.

How could such a passage possibly support the exalting of Jewish flesh over the Gentile, and a return to the Old Testament dispensation? If it pleases the premillennialists to ignore the necessary spiritualising of this allegorical passage, whilst spiritualising the seventy weeks of Daniel till it is distorted beyond all recognition, that is one thing. But to overturn the doctrines of grace is another.

The way in which they have elasticated Daniel's seventy weeks is beyond the stretching of all imagination. They expand sixty nine weeks (of years) from Daniel to the coming of Christ. But the last, seventieth, week, they make

15

the tribulation period of Rev. ch. 4-19! But what of the continuing period of two thousand years in time between the coming of Christ—that is, at the end of the sixty nine 'weeks'—and the final future seventieth 'week' waiting to be fulfilled at the end of the present age?

What of it? Oh, no problem at all, it is shrugged off with nonchalance by people to whom what is logical or reasonable bears no relation to what they dogmatize. But is it not putting deception into the mouth of the Lord, to state that when God says seventy weeks—of years—he means nothing like it, because from Pentecost to the Second coming is treated as irrelevant, not counted, it does not exist, it is a void, the seventieth week is to be joined to the sixty ninth, as though the intervening two thousand years of time—so far—were nothing?

Is this honest dealing with Jews who counted seventy weeks from Daniel till the coming of Messiah? Simeon did not so count. They shall bear their judgment for such slipshod public accounting of our absent Lord's business, in the day of reckoning.

10. The Cross

In like manner the premillennialists undermine the cross, the judgment of the world, and the condemnation of the flesh, by their exalting of Jewish flesh to a place of millennial pre-eminence. But no flesh, Jewish or other-wise, should glory in his presence. They put a lie in the apostle's mouth, who said that between Jew and Gentile, 'There is no difference', by saying, There is a difference. Who, think ye, is right?

Paul says 'Circumcision profiteth nothing', they say, It profiteth everything. But who speaks the truth, do you think? As to Christ's slaying the enmity of the flesh by the cross, to make of Jew and Gentile one new man, they resurrect that flesh, and overturn the cross.

Though in the days of the New Testament the Jewish saints gained an interest in Christ by believing, in the so-called 'tribulation' they gain it by working. Though Paul once counted Jewishness gain, now he counts it dung and dross. They, however, esteem it better than gold, yea, than much fine gold.

In this millennium of theirs God is expected to exalt what Paul calls dung and dross, over the whole earth. And what the apostles' counted as better than gold, yea, than much fine gold, they expect the Lord to cast upon the millennial dung-heap.

11. Eating with Gentiles

When Paul saw Peter refusing to eat with the Gentiles, because he would eat with the Jews only, he rebuked him for not walking uprightly according to the truth of the gospel, Gal. 2:14. But in this fictitious millennium, when the ceremonial law is reintroduced, if a Jew eats with a Gentile he breaks the law, thus justifying Peter, condemning Paul, and causing the gospel to be trodden underfoot to suit these fantastic notions.

Galatians 2:18 informs us that if we build again the legal covenant of works and ceremonies, we become transgressors, destroying the work of Christ. But these make God do it, and their excuse is that he does it in their mythical hole in time and space, though it should overturn the dispensations, trample the gospel, reintroduce the law of commandments contained in ordinances, and manifest again what had for ever vanished away. No matter, provided dispensational premillennialism be the reason for changing and reversing the sworn truth of God.

12. The Legal System

The premillennialists will have the temple rebuilt, sacrifices reintroduced, ceremonial law re-established, in a word, the Old Covenant returned. They will have Jews saved by bowing to Messiah their glorified King. As opposed to believing the truth of the gospel. That is, saved by a legal look on the outward appearance. In a word, by effects and works. By an external view of Messiah so powerful that it would quell every natural opposition—for the time being—by fear and amazement.

Clearly, such a reign would be so materially advantageous to the Jew that, on this ground alone, none would reject it. 'Lord, evermore give us this bread.'

The premillennialist has no thought of the operations of the Holy Ghost on the heart, of believing the gospel spiritually, of looking to Golgotha from a broken and contrite spirit, of vital union with the living vine. It is all 'salvation' by an exterior assent to a kingly glory on the ground of Jewish flesh and blood.

Yet from the beginning it was not of blood, nor of the will of the flesh, nor of the will of man, but of God. Now, however, it is of Israelite blood, it is of the will of Hebrew flesh, and it is of the will of Jewish man, without God at all, save by outward appearances.

This overturns the gospel completely, as it does true Judaism. For 'he is not a Jew which is one outwardly, neither is that circumcision which is outward in the flesh.' Except in the millennium. Jesus said, 'Except a man be born again he cannot see the kingdom of God.' But these see, it since they are born Jews. Thus they make nothing of Jesus' word, because in the millennium they see the kingdom of God without being born again.

13. The Law

In Galatians 2:19, Paul was dead to the law, being crucified with Christ. But, whilst glorified, he hovers above, seeing the word which the Holy Ghost gave to him to stand for ever, fall to the ground below. In the gospel according to premillennialism the law is reintroduced, and both the death of Christ, and the saints' death with Christ, are undone. Jews are alive to the law with a witness, animal sacrifices are brought in, a levitical service is performed and legal obligation is contracted.

Paul, helpless in the glory, glorified in the body, must watch men below in the body of sin contradicting everything he had been given of God as gospel world without end.

As to righteousness coming by the law—to which the millennial Jew must submit—if righteousness come by the law then Christ is dead in vain. Now see where this error has led them. They make vain the death of Christ, because no word of honour, no promise, no oath, no vow, no truth, matters one whit if turned to a lie in a mythical dispensation.

Moreover Gal. 3:7 tells us that they that are of faith are the children of Abraham. But these make the children of the flesh the children of Abraham, of whom the Spirit testifies, 'these are not the children', Rom. 9:8.

We are assured, Gal. 3:10, that they that are under the works of the law are under a curse. But in the millennium blessing and cursing are reversed, for, taken from the gospel, the Jews will be under the law in order to obtain the blessing. The law is not of faith, says Gal. 3:12, and no man is justified by it. Then why bring it—or any part of it—back again in the millennium? If Christ hath redeemed us from the curse of the law, being made a curse for us, that the blessing of Abraham might come on the Gentiles, and that by faith, how is it that the blessing, without faith, falls upon the natural children of the flesh, the Jews, and that by works?

And if the law cannot disannul the gospel, Gal. 3:17, how can these Jews be saved by a Messiah reintroducing levitical law, without the gospel? For premillennialists say, It is not the gospel in the millennium, but the recognition and bowing to Christ as Messiah, as son of David, as king. No word of Son of God, no word of the gospel of the grace of God. But much of law. But, saith God, it cannot disannul the gospel. But says the premillennialist, it can. Then he adds, *sotto voce*, aside, It is only levitical law. Only? Then what of the sacrifices? Oh, they are commemorative. What, a memorial required, with five glorified scars before their faces?

14. The Levitical Offerings

No sacrifice is commemorative, it is a contradiction in terms. Sacrifices are a substitutionary atonement offered by a priest on behalf of an offerer, to expiate sin and propitiate God. Sacrifices are nothing else whatsoever. Such euphemisms as 'commorative' do not alter the real character of the thing. Such deceitful prevarication serves no purpose but to disguise the reality, becloud the judgment, and beg the issue.

Oh, they say, But their gospel is not the gospel as we have it. Then it is another gospel. And if another gospel then the god of this world has invented it, and the terrible thing is, premillennialism has brought it in. Is it not of faith? Then it is of works. It is not the gospel.

When the Jews were 'children', they were under bondage to the elements of this world. The law was their schoolmaster to lead them to Christ. But in the millennium Christ is their schoolmaster to lead them to the law, to sacrifices of constantly slaughtered carcases, and to rivers of blood running at Jerusalem. All this, to expiate sin and propitiate a God who is supposed to have appointed his Son to oversee this contemptuous dismissal of the gospel, performed by day and by night, in full view of his glorified scars bearing witness to a work of which he had said, 'It is finished'.

Then, Jews must be sanctified by levitical ministrations. The disobedient Jew who repudiates the sacrifices, rejects priestly levitical service, refuses the Jewish ceremonies, abjures works, in a word, who obeys the apostle, would be cut off from his people. Why? Because he has no faith? No, because he has faith, and, by it, he refuses works. Tell me, what sort of a scheme is this?

Meanwhile the poor Gentile is put down, the Jew exalted, the middle wall of partition, which had been removed by the cross, is raised again, and the cross thereby diminished. If a poor Gentile found a Bible—which is unlikely, if Jewish interests are to be served—and read therein 'there is neither Jew nor Greek: for ye are all one in Christ Jesus. And if ye be Christ's, then are ye Abraham's seed', Gal. 3:28-29, straightway the fleshly seed of Abraham would laugh him to scorn, and admonish him not to expect such nonsense as that in the millennium. And if he remonstrated, they would refuse to bring him to Messiah, effectually cutting off his hope of salvation.

15. The Seed of Abraham

It is written, Gal. 4:22-26, that Abraham had two sons, one by the bondwoman, the other by the free. One born of the flesh, the other by promise.

Each signified a covenant, the first at Sinai, in bondage with her children, pertaining to earthly Jerusalem, which answers to Hagar's seed. Now this is the Jerusalem of the premillennialists, called by John, Sodom and Egypt. But they will exalt her up to the skies, over all the earth, as if to honour their own mother. Despite the fact that, Gal. 4:21, she is in bondage to the old yoke, bringing her children under the curse of the law, the damning sentence, and the killing letter.

To glorify this earthly Jerusalem, called Sodom and Egypt, where our Lord was crucified, they would bring Christ down from above, whither the premillennialists ascend to fetch him. And shall Christ bring in what it cost him his life to take out?

But this is with the gospel, they prate. Oh? they said it was not the gospel. But only not as we know it. Then, another gospel. And another gospel will not change the character of Jerusalem below, in bondage with her children. No more will Christ, despite all their frustrated efforts to make him do their will and reign there.

But Christ reigns in Jerusalem above: out of Zion, the perfection of beauty, hath God shined. This is free Jerusalem, the mother of us all, and none other. These

Jerusalems are in opposition, they are utterly in contrast one with the other, as are the two covenants, law and grace, works and faith. Here is immutable, everlasting opposition. And let not premillennialists join together what God hath put asunder, lest he come and smite them with the rod of his mouth.

As to these Jews—regarding the millennium—we wot not what is become of them. But at the time now present we solemnly admonish them to believe the gospel in this dispensation, for there is none in any other.

Millennialists require us to receive the testimony of still waiting Jews. But why are they waiting? Because they deny Christ's deity, mock at the Trinity, stumble at the cross, reject the righteousness of God, blaspheme the Holy Ghost, and despise the gospel.

The millennialists assist them by ignoring all these things as if they were of no account. The meanwhile they confuse God's house with earthly temples, Jerusalem above with Jerusalem below, the crucified body with reinstated flesh, the sacrificial atonement with reintroduced sacrifices, and the priesthood for ever after the order of Melchizedek with the levitical priesthood finally passed away.

God has declared, and declared once and for all, 'If ye be circumcised, Christ shall profit you nothing', Gal. 5:2. There is not now, nor ever shall be, any salvation except by the free grace of the gospel. Neither is there any access to grace other than by faith. Nor is there the least grain of true faith but by the Holy Ghost in the regeneration. If the foundations be destroyed, what shall the righteous do?

16. Priesthood

We are assured, I Tim. 2:5, that there is one mediator between God and men, the man Christ Jesus. Then what are these mediatorial levitical priests—mediating, incidentally, between angels and men—in this fabled millenium? They are offering 'memorial' sacrifices. Like the memorial sacrifice of the Mass, is it? A continuing of the Roman priesthood in principle, is it? With a reversion to slaughtered animal sacrifices?

Priests are priests, and sacrifices are sacrifices, and either there is a need for them, or there is no need for them.

If Christ's sacrifice is now found to be deficient, then those sacrifices might be required. If his priesthood proved inadequate, he might delegate to other priests. But if fault were found with the levitical priesthood, if Christ be sworn with an oath a priest for ever, if his sacrifice be perfect, obtaining eternal redemption for those for whom it was made, if he be the one and only mediator between God and men, then what kind of blasphemy is it to put levitical priests and sacrifices between the Jews and him?

Heb. 5:6 declares that Christ is a priest for ever after the order of Melchidezek. This dismisses in perpetuity the levitical priesthood, a priesthood for a brief dying lifetime under the imperfect order of Aaron. They came in by the law of a carnal commandment, but he by the power of an endless life. They were appointed by Moses, but he by the oath of God for evermore. Their sacrifices were repetitive, his was once and for all. 'For by one offering he hath perfected for ever them that are sanctified.'

The failed levitical priests, with their ineffectual sacrifices, are what the premillennialists foist upon Almighty God during their millennium. They are memorial sacrifices? They are nonetheless sacrifices for that. No matter how the premillennialists might twist and turn to evade the pointed sword of God's word, mitigating their priesthood by disguising their sacrifices, priesthood is always priesthood, and sacrifices are always sacrifices. They say that levitical priesthood will be re-established. If so, violating God's oath, dismissing God's priest, despising God's sacrifice, annulling God's word, and procuring the evil inventions of a churl, Isa. 32:7.

And shall the levitical priesthood be restored at any time? Then, Heb. 7:11, since perfection was not by the levitical priesthood, under which the people received the law which brought bondage, which cursed them with a curse, even that whole nation, I say, since perfection was not by it, what of the discovered need of another priest after the order of Melchizedek? He should bring in perfection, and that, Heb. 7:12, through a change of the law.

By the same token, if there is seen in the millennium a further need of the levitical priesthood, and thus a return to the law, it must be because perfection was not obtained by God's Melchizedek after all. Is this their charge? If not, why do they wish to bring back the Levites? Since they served, by definition, under the law, bringing them back argues of necessity bringing back the law under which they served.

But if there be a disannulling of the covenant going before for the weakness and unprofitableness thereof, Heb. 7:18, because it made nothing perfect, Heb. 7:19, and could not bring to God, but only to condemnation, has the gospel failed, under which Melchizedek serves, that they must require God to bring back what had been for ever disannulled?

If the gospel has failed them, it has not failed me, and they should look well to their doctrine of the gospel, if they have any, for if it is anything like their doctrine of the last things, it shall surely fail them, and they shall go to their Maker with a lie in their right hand.

17. The Sacrifices

As to the animal sacrifices under the law, they were, Heb. 9:9, a figure for the time then present. Not of the premillennial time to come. And if they could not then make the offerer perfect, as pertaining to the conscience, why memorialise that?

If they say, No, it is a memorial to Christ, I answer, The bread and wine are that. But then, the bread and wine were given to the church, not to a reinstated Israel after the church is raptured. And given, observe, as a memorial only 'till he come', not after he has come.

A sacrifice, however, cannot be a memorial, it is an offering to God, through death, for an atonement. Why then will the Jews sacrifice, and so insult the Lamb of God? But they say, No, it is a memorial for them, as is the supper for us. Then we repeat, If the Lord's supper be the memorial, why do they not use it?

The sacrifices are never called memorial, nor could they be. They are an ineffectual, inadequate, imperfect type: a blood-soaked figure till the true should come. Now that the antitype, the substance, has come, that which was imperfect is done away, the shadows are for ever gone.

If they reintroduce shadows it is clear to us all that they have blocked out the light. But with God there is no shadow cast by turning. If levitical sacrifices are made to come in again, verily God must appear to turn back to that which had waxed old, which had perished, which was done away, because, after all, that which is perfect proved inadequate in the issue. Can that be right?

18. The Temple

But they rebuild the temple too! To that the shadowy levitical sacrificial service pertained. But Christ having come, and having offered up one sacrifice once for all, the priesthood pertains to a greater and more perfect tabernacle, not made with hands. Into this perfect tabernacle Christ entered, rending the veil from the top to the bottom, passing high into the heavenlies, having obtained eternal redemption for us.

Eternal redemption? If eternal, why a thousand years of shadows restored? Why the worldly tabernacle rebuilt? Why the levitical priesthood reinstated? Why the animal sacrifices reintroduced?

If the shadowy animal sacrifices, Heb. 10:1-2, could not make the comers thereunto perfect—for then would they not have ceased to be offered?—the cessation of offering is witness to the coming of a perfect and eternal sacrifice. But equally, the resumption of the old shadowy sacrifices, must bear witness to imperfection found in that by which they were done away at the first.

And now where is the premillennialist? The resumption of animal sacrifices in a repetitive sequence is a clear testimony that the sacrifice of Christ has proved inadequate to do away with them after all. No other conclusion can be reached by such a resumption.

Then, the atonement of Christ is dismissed, the blood of Christ degraded, and eternal redemption is brought into question. There can be no excuse for such a system as this.

How have the premillennialists got themselves into such an error? Because once having adopted the position that the Old Testament prophecies concerning the future blessing of Israel and Judah are literal, and not spiritual, inevitably they have trapped themselves into enormities the consequences of which they refuse to consider.

Why refuse? Because it would force them at once to see that their position is wholly untenable, and must be renounced. This would require a fairness, a humility, and a willingness to respond that is, astonishingly, at its rarest among those who pride themselves upon being what they consider most scriptural. But they are not scriptural at all, much less are they spiritual. Such people are merely traditional, with a blindness quite equal to that of the Jews.

19. The Prophecies

It is not merely obvious, nor only spiritual, but wholly essential that the Old Testament prophecies of Israel's and of Judah's future blessing should be spiritualised.

The chosen Gentiles must be seen as Abraham's seed by faith, the believer as the inward Jew, and the people collectively as the Israel of God, circumcised in heart and ears, the lawful heirs to the promises made unto the fathers.

The alternative to spiritualising the prophecies is to literalise them: and we have seen where that inevitably leads the premillennialist. He finds himself, however unintentionally, the advocate of a system which tears down the edifice of grace, contradicts the gospel, and tramples underfoot the Son of God in a humiliating millennial reign of confusion.

Refusing the true, the spiritual, interpretation of the prophecies, taking the prophets to refer to the carnal Jews, Israel after the flesh, the premillennialists are forced into the position of finding an age into which to fit their interpretation, after Christ's second coming.

The convenience of the singular passage graphically portraying the symbol of a thousand years in Revelation chapter 20 immediately appears. This allegory is therefore leaped upon with utmost relief, and, their argument being so strained and weak, held on to with frenzied tenacity.

Without such absurd abuse of the three or four verses of pictorial imagery in Revelation chapter 20, they would be lost in their carnal and unspiritual literalising of Old Testament prophecy. With it, they are able to save their faces. But what do any of our faces matter? It is the truth that matters.

If the prophecies in the Old Testament, which premillennialists multiply but never properly interpret, I say, if the prophecies are not read as spiritually fulfilled in this present age for the children of Abraham by faith, that is, believing Gentiles, all is cast into absurdity and worse. No matter how vivid the language of the prophet in terms then understood, however Jewish the imagery of the seer, if it is not spiritualized—to answer to the people of God today, the true Israel—then the Old Testament is made to overthrow the New, law to overturn grace, and Christ is ultimately insulted and degraded in his person and sacrifice beyond toleration and endurance.

20. The Conclusion

As to the whole Old Testament, with its entire priesthood, sacrifices, temple, and legal system, 'He taketh away the first, that he may establish the second', Heb. 10:9. This taking away signifies the removal of the sacrifices once and for all: they are taken away absolutely, never to be reintroduced in any form whatsoever.

'That he may establish the second.' This denotes the foundation of Jesus Christ and him crucified. It is the sacrifice of the body of Jesus once and for all. It answers to the Lamb of God, who by one offering perfected for ever them that are sanctified. This he established eternally, in place of the former, which was temporal, which he takes out of the way for evermore.

Forasmuch as Christ's one sacrifice endureth, in no wise can the former be re-established in any form at all, or under any circumstances whatever, without overturning the word of God. Such a thing would deny the oath of God, and make a mockery of God's veracity and truthfulness.

This would, and it must, bring in confusion worse confounded, joining both covenants, and uniting both Jerusalems. It would build up into one communion the bond-child and the freeborn, Sinai and Zion, law and gospel, works and faith, Hagar and Sarah, Christ and Belial. It would bind opposites together in an alliance more unholy than the mystery of iniquity, because uniting all that God had separated and denying everything that the deity had asserted.

The truth is, every saved Hebrew is not come, nor ever will come, to the mount that might be touched, from which both animal sacrifices and worldly tabernacle were given, which answered to Jerusalem below. But every spiritual Jew will come, and must come, the whole seed of Abraham by faith shall come, as the true Israel of God, the fulfilment of Israel and Judah in spirit, I say, shall come to the mount which is above.

'Every one of them appeareth before God in Zion.' They shall come to spiritual Zion, to the city of the living God, to the heavenly Jerusalem, that is, to mount Zion above.

As to the present world, this age, the earth that now is, it shall be shaken, and the land of Israel with it, and not the earth only, but the heavens also. So shall all things that are made be utterly removed. But we, having received a kingdom which cannot be moved, and having received it by grace alone, through faith only, doing the will of God, shall abide forever.

Such as be of faith are spiritual Sarah's offspring, the children of the promise, the true seed of Abraham, the Israel of God. They have come to the blood of sprinkling, which speaketh better things than that of Abel. This is that people to whom pertains the promised inheritance, sure to all the seed, not of a typical land of Canaan, but of the antitypical world to come, of which we speak.

At the one, and only, return and second coming of Christ, raised from the dead, all such shall hear this word from the Lord of Glory, the Son of God, Jesus Christ himself: 'Come, ye blessed of my Father, inherit the kingdom prepared for you from the foundation of the world.' That is, a Kingdom established by grace, through righteousness, in the world to come, never to be removed, world without end. Amen.

THE END

Order Form

Please send to the address below:-

		Price	Quantity
A Question for Pope John Paul II		£1.25	......
Of God or Man?		£1.45	......
Noah and the Flood		£1.20	......
Divine Footsteps		£0.40	......
The Red Heifer		£0.75	......
The Wells of Salvation		£1.50	......

Psalms, Hymns & Spiritual Songs (Hardback edition)

		Price	Quantity
The Psalms of the Old Testament		£2.50	......
Spiritual Songs from the Gospels		£2.50	......
The Hymns of the New Testament		£2.50	......

'Apostolic Foundation of the Christian Church' series

		Price	Quantity
Foundations Uncovered	Vol.I	£0.30	......
The Birth of Jesus Christ	Vol.II	£0.95	......
The Messiah	Vol.III	£2.45	......
The Son of God and Seed of David	Vol.IV	£1.10	......

Tracts

		Price	Quantity
The Two Prayers of Elijah		£0.10	......
Wounded for our Transgressions		£0.10	......
The Blood of Sprinkling		£0.10	......
The Grace of God that Brings Salvation		£0.10	......

'Tract for the Times' series

		Price	Quantity
The Gospel of God	No.1	£0.25	......
The Strait Gate	No.2	£0.25	......
Eternal Sonship and Taylor Brethren	No.3	£0.25	......
Marks of the New Testament Church	No.4	£0.25	......
The Charismatic Delusion	No.5	£0.25	......
Premillennialism Exposed	No.6	£0.25	......
Justification and Peace	No.7	£0.25	......
Faith or presumption?	No.8	£0.25	......

Name and Address (in block capitals)

. . . .

. . . .

If money is sent with order please allow for postage. Please address to:- The John Metcalfe Publishing Trust, Church Road, Tylers Green, Penn, Bucks, HP10 8LN.

THE MINISTRY OF THE NEW TESTAMENT

The purpose of this 32 page A4 gloss paper magazine is to provide spiritual and experimental ministry with sound doctrine which rightly and prophetically divides the Word of Truth.

Readers of our books will already know the high standards of our publications. They can be confident that these pages will maintain that quality, by giving access to enduring ministry from the past, and publishing a living ministry from the present.

Order Form

Name and Address (in block capitals)

. . . .

. . . .

. . . .

Please send me .... copies of The Ministry of the New Testament.

Please send me .... year/s subscription.

I enclose a cheque/postal order for £ ....

(Price: including postage,
U.K. £1.75; Overseas £1.90)
(One year's subscription: Including postage,
U.K. £7.00; Overseas £7.60)

Cheques should be made payable to The John Metcalfe Publishing Trust, and for overseas subscribers should be in pounds sterling drawn on a London Bank.

10 or more copies to one address will qualify for a 10% discount

Please send to The John Metcalfe Publishing Trust, Church Road, Tylers Green, Penn, Bucks, HP10 8LN

All Publications of the Trust are subsidised by the Publishers.